Keeping It Together

Linking Reading Theory and Practice

Ian Morrison

Contents

INTRODUCTION

A previous publication, *Getting It Together,* (Morrison, 1993) explores a consistent link between sound reading theory and consequent appropriate practice. *Keeping It Together* seeks to expand upon this view in a practical way.

Keeping It Together enlarges upon the concept of strategy-based teaching, using mainly non age-graded material. This book details how to begin, and subsequently plan, a program, effective use of available resources, and the best use of limited teacher time.

Keeping It Together examines the issues surrounding teaching children with reading difficulties, and how to affect change in colleagues.

Teachers who already hold a similar view of the reading process will be able to use this book to further their development. For teachers who are just beginning to consider whole language, or literature-based reading programs, *Keeping It Together* moves carefully through the issues, allowing teachers to grasp the topics at their own pace.

1. BEGINNING THE PROCESS

For some teachers, using a strategy-based approach to the teaching of reading will be a huge step. For others, it will be a natural consequence, growing out of a more child-centred approach to learning in general. However, for most teachers, there are four major areas to consider before beginning the school year:

- Your own view of the reading process.
- The policies within your institution.
- The resources that are available.
- The records that have been accumulated about children's reading behaviour.

Your View of the Process

The first issue that must be addressed is your own view of how children learn to read. Although it is not necessary to be fully convinced that children learn to read by reading real books, in order to get started, it *is* important that one at least holds this as an assumption, and analyses children's reading in the light of it. You need to feel confident that children will learn to read if the right conditions are in place. In some cases, this will require a reassessment of the traditional views of the process. Above all, the teacher needs to keep an open mind and be a keen observer of what children are *really* doing as they read.

Institutional Policies

Institutional policy can be a difficult area. What we *wish* to do as teachers, and what we are *able* to do within existing policy, may be in conflict. For example, you may be becoming increasingly convinced that a strategy-based approach to the teaching of reading has much merit, yet your school or district may have a policy that outlines a different approach. The extent of this gulf will differ from school to school, district to district, and country to country.

In some cases, it will not be an easy task to convince administrators to allow you to "give it a go". This is why it is important for teachers to be knowledgeable and articulate about the reading process. Chapter 5 discusses some of the issues involved in working with other teachers and administrators.

Available Resources

Before beginning a strategy-based reading program, the teacher will need to gather as much reading material as possible. This material should incorporate a wide selection of genres and styles, including fantasy, fiction, non-fiction, narrative, informational and so on. So called *reading age* should only be a minor consideration. As will be seen later, the difficulty of any particular book or passage can be determined by what the teacher does with it. However, having said this, it would still be useful to arrange material loosely into half-year age levels. Quantity and quality are the keys here. It is not necessary to stick to one publisher's list.

In fact this is counter-productive, as the publications may assume a different view of the reading process. The goal is to expose children to varied and meaningful texts, as opposed to contrived and controlled language.

Records of Reading Behaviour

At the beginning of the year, records of the children's reading behaviour from the previous year can sometimes be useful, but often misleading. Information stated purely in terms of reading age or *sub-skills*, such as *word attack*, are at best of minimal value. One problem is that reading age is variable and often quite unreliable. A second problem is that the sub-skills of reading may not tell the teacher anything meaningful about how the child processes print. A third problem is that the summer break brings changes in what children can do. A much more useful set of data is information about how children process print. This would include an analysis of the strategies children use when reading.

What cues are used for prediction? What checking behaviours are evident? Does the child re-read to confirm, or pick up more information? This material will be much more useful in setting up an appropriate program.

Beginning the School Year

Before the children have arrived, the teacher has made some commitment to a strategy-based approach to teaching reading, obtained at least partial backing from school administrators, assembled a comprehensive range of reading materials, and looked carefully at *appropriate* records of reading behaviour. The next task is to plan the first two weeks. The major goal throughout this time is to assess individual children's reading behaviour. In certain situations, another goal may be to convince children that they are in fact learning to read as they read. We are referring here to children who are accustomed to programs that emphasise phonic skills, the rote learning of words, or a work book approach, for example. This may also be a good time to introduce the approach to the children's parents or caregivers (see Morrison, 1993, p. 53).

The First Two Weeks

As you begin a new year it is important to consider more than a review of last year's learning. In order to understand the process children use to make sense of text, it is necessary that you have accurate data on how the children process print as quickly as possible. This requires the freeing-up of teacher time, and implies that the children need to be engaged in tasks that require a minimum of teacher monitoring.

It is beyond the scope of this book to deal effectively with classroom management and behaviour issues.

Teachers will have developed their own ways of establishing routines in the first few days. However, it is important that set routines are established *before* beginning your program.

One useful way of starting the program — and freeing-up teacher time — is to have a topic or unit so thoroughly prepared, that it virtually runs itself. Of course, the amount of preparation involved, and the degree of freedom afforded, will largely depend upon the ages of the children. For senior children a contract may be appropriate, involving children being able to choose from a range of activities around a theme, for example, "friends". The tasks could include activities such as: portrait painting of an ideal friend, writing a profile of a friend, reading teacher-assembled books about friends, researching material on friendship, and so on. At a more junior level, activities could include: listening to a taped story, magazine research for friendly pictures, constructing a collage of friendly words, writing stories "I like ... because ...", and so on. Creative teachers will construct their own set of activities. Initial preparation, acquisition of resources, and good routines will become very important and require careful consideration.

By beginning with a topic study or unit, the teacher can start to display the belief that learning takes place when the task is whole and meaningful. At no stage during this time will children be engaged in isolated tasks, meaningless drills, or rote learning. Whatever time is freed-up — and this will differ from one situation to the next — is time that can be spent in assessing the children's reading behaviour.

The Initial Assessment

With an average class size of 30, a teacher needs to plan to assess three children per day to have the required information to begin the program at the end of the second week. In some cases, the assessment may take longer, which is not a problem as the children will still be learning from their unit work. It is crucial that the teacher ensures he or she has made a preliminary assessment of every child, before implementing program strategies.

Assessment Measures

The most important measure, and the one that when analysed will reveal the most useful information, is the *Running Record* (Clay, 1985). If this is unavailable, it is suggested that teachers use *Miscue Analysis* (Goodman, 1973). The goal is to find some text that the child can read at an *instructional* level. For the purposes of this book, instructional level is viewed as word reading accuracy of between 90% and 95%. This is generally the area where the behaviour is most likely to reveal what the child is attempting to do. When the accuracy is higher, there tends not to be enough behaviour to analyse. When the accuracy level gets below 90%, the good behaviours often break down.

Approximate *age-level* data from the previous year can be a good source of where to begin finding appropriate material. However, because children change, and text difficulty is often unreliable, the teacher may need to take two or three running records before getting one at the appropriate level. Teachers who are unsure of the steps they should take in administering a running record should refer to the Appendix.

The Analysis

The analysis can be as simple or as complex as the teacher feels capable of. The teacher does not need to be an expert in this area to begin. The expertise will increase as more running records are analysed. Any reliable information is better than none at all.

After getting a running record at an appropriate level of difficulty, it becomes a matter of asking questions about what the child appears to be doing as he or she reads. These questions are as follows:

- Does the child use meaning or semantic cues? (M)
- Does the child use structural or syntactic cues? (S)
- Does the child use visual or graphophonic cues? (V)
- How does the child use these cues to predict text?
- How does the child use these cues to check on predictions?
- Generally, how does the child monitor his or her reading?
- Does the child re-read to confirm predictions?
- Does the child take the initiative to search further when meaning breaks down?
- Is there a high rate of self-correction? (SC)
- Is the reading fluent and with expression?

With some practice, the teacher will be able to establish what the child is doing well, and what he or she is having difficulty with. This information will become the basis for beginning to plan the program.

If the teacher is fortunate enough to have similar information from a previous year, it is an interesting and useful exercise to compare the two sets. There may be some insight into what the child learned over the break. At this stage of the year, the teacher now has enough information with which to begin planning a strategy-based program. The next chapters will concentrate on the elements of a strategy-based program, and deal with planning, running, and monitoring the program.

2. STRATEGY-BASED TEACHING

Getting It Together (Morrison, 1993) introduced the concept of strategy-based teaching. This chapter seeks to expand upon the concept; defining the term, and explaining how the teacher can foster various strategies.

Strategy based teaching of reading involves the teacher working with a group of children on a particular reading strategy. The make-up of the group will be determined by a careful analysis of running records.

Purpose and Balance

Before linking specific strategies with specific teaching, we must sound a note of caution. The effective use of strategies involves using appropriate reading behaviours in an orchestrated fashion. So, it is very important to recognise that the isolation of specific strategies for teaching needs to be seen as a temporary measure, and used when there is a very clear reason to do so.

If children learn to read by reading, then it is suggested that children need to be grouped in two different ways. These will be referred to as *strategy grouping* and *mileage grouping*. It is important to strike a balance between the two types of groups. In summary, the teacher needs to be clear about why he or she is working with a specific group at any one time.

Strategy Grouping

Within any good, balanced, reading program, there will be a range of teaching techniques used, including reading-to children, shared reading, guided reading, independent reading, language experience, and writing. The most powerful lessons will contain a combination of these techniques. Although it could be argued that a good teacher may use any of the above techniques to foster many of the strategies, some elements of the balanced reading program are more suited to the fostering of particular strategies. The strategies we will be concentrating on are as follows:

- Developing the use of meaning cues.
- Developing the use of structural cues.
- Developing the use of visual cues.
- Integrating cue use in prediction and checking.
- Re-reading and reading-on.
- Developing fluency and expression.

Developing the Use of Meaning Cues

Because reading is a meaning-driven activity, the most important consideration for the teacher is to ensure that children use meaning cues well; that they see text reading as a meaningful experience. Most children will either arrive at school with this understanding, or quickly pick it up. However, some children will require a greater concentration in this area.

Daily *reading-to* children text that is meaningful is an excellent start, and time should be set aside for whole class sessions. Children can easily *hear* that text makes sense, and the teacher can provide a model that clearly indicates that it also makes sense for him or her. To further enhance the point, the teacher may wish to pause in certain places and allow the children to complete the phrase. However, this can be a problem if it is overdone, as there is a risk of the children loosing the overall meaning of the selection.

A *shared reading* lesson can be useful for establishing the use of meaning cues. The teacher needs to select an enlarged book in which the text is fairly predictable. When the teacher has read it through once to the children, they can join in on a second reading. On the second reading, the teacher will cover up some highly predictable words. It is suggested that the entire word is covered up, as the goal is the use of meaning cues. Often, children who are not using meaning cues well, are also excessively concerned with the use of visual cues. By covering the entire word, children are encouraged to use meaning cues. It is essential that the teacher accept any word from the child that makes sense, even when it is not the correct word. The goal is to convince children that what is already in their heads is as important as what is on the page.

When children begin to respond consistently well to the shared reading experience, there should be a carryover effect in their own reading of recreational material. The discussion so far has been aimed at the word level. As we will see later, *guided reading* can be very helpful with longer stretches of meaning.

Developing the Use of Structural Cues

Because meaning and structure are so closely linked, errors that children make are not often meaningful without also being structurally appropriate. It is difficult to generate examples where the meaning is clear, but the language structure is incorrect, for example:

```
    going
   ----------
We  go   to   the   zoo.
```

This situation most commonly arises with children for whom English is not their first language, and children who come to school with a limited command of oral language. It is beyond the scope of this book, and the expertise of the author, to deal with this area in any detail, however, the following points need to be considered. Because skilled readers use the *redundancy* (Smith, 1985) in meaning, language structure, and visual cues, to eliminate prior alternatives, these children are at a disadvantage. It is important to avoid the temptation to delay reading instruction, and work first upon oral language. Children do not acquire literacy skills in a linear fashion.

Because these children need to hear the sounds of the English language, *reading-to* and *shared reading* can be very useful vehicles for promoting the use of structural cues. The benefits of massive amounts of reading-to are obvious. However, during *shared reading,* the teacher needs to concentrate more upon *multiple* readings of the text, to get the sounds of language into the children's heads. Text needs to be carefully chosen, and it is suggested that teachers avoid uncommon or irregular language patterns. These children need lots of time to practice on text that contains similar structures. Notwithstanding the above, these children need opportunities to hear correct forms of the English language, and the teacher needs to set aside time to talk with them.

Developing the Use of Visual Cues

This is an area that is fraught with pitfalls. How often have you heard it said, or perhaps said it yourself: "You should know that word, I taught it!" The difficulty is that children don't learn words in isolation. Granted, it is useful for children to have a small store of high-frequency words that they recognise easily and consistently, but new words are learned within meaningful context. It is not necessary to "know" a word in every detail to be able to read it, and in fact children who excessively concentrate upon detail run the risk of losing meaning, as their reading slows down. We all know children who read "look" for "like" and "like" for "look", when presented with a word list, but never make the same mistakes when the words are in context.

Children need to know just enough about how words work, in order to combine meaning and structural cues, to make accurate predictions, or to check on predictions already made. Children do not need to learn lists of words in isolation, nor do they need to have difficult words pre-taught. The pre-teaching of words denies the child the opportunity of processing cues, and perhaps getting it right. Nor is *sounding-out* the answer. Sounding out doesn't bring the reader closer to meaning, unless the child already has the word in her head. If the child does already have the word in his or her head, then sounding out is a very low level and cumbersome strategy. In this case, the child needs to use meaning and structural cues and a quick scan of the dominant features of the word.

Having said this, there are children who use meaning and structural cues well, but tend to neglect visual cues. Specifically constructed *shared reading* lessons can be useful in this situation. The goal is to have the children pick up just enough detail to confirm their prediction. Again, using an enlarged book, the teacher can mask specific words where the meaning is clear, for example:

Goldilocks scampered through the __________.

The teacher's task is to invite predictions, then ask what letters children would expect to see at the beginning and the end, and then to uncover the word. For children who have difficulty predicting a meaningful word, the teacher can supply 3 or 4 possibilities that are meaningful, but clearly different with respect to how they look, for example, *forest*, *woods*, and *trees*. When the children are comfortable with this, the teacher can increase the difficulty of the task, for example, using *forest, field* and *foliage*. The key here is that this takes place within the context of meaningful print, and that children use only as much information as necessary.

Certainly an understanding of how words work will help with reading. Children who are able to recognise chunks, syllabify, and see relationships between words, will be able to check predictions more accurately. However, these are skills which children learn as an outcome of reading. It is often argued that high progress readers have better word skills, and therefore teaching these skills is important. This is largely a chicken and egg argument. What children who are having some difficulty in this area need is to read more, not isolated drills.

There is however, one area where children need to be proficient in the use of visual cues, and that is in *writing*. This is the area that teachers can concentrate upon all those word exercises that used to be taken during reading. When children write, they already control the use of meaning and language structure, that is they know what they are going to write about. This frees up the child to concentrate on the sound to letter area. By keeping the focus on the use of visual cues during writing, children are learning the skills they need in reading, while avoiding an over reliance on the visual cue area while reading.

Integrating the Use of Prediction and Checking

This section discusses the integration of cues, both at the word level, and for larger chunks of text.

At the word level, the goal is to help children to use a variety of cues to predict, and to check upon their predictions. Some children tend to rely more heavily on the use of a particular cue, and then have difficulty in checking to see if they are correct. Often, children in the beginning stages of reading will use meaning and structural cues with only limited reference to visual cues. Older readers who are having some difficulty with reading often do the opposite; attempt to use visual cues without checking on meaning. The former is much easier to deal with.

In a *shared reading* lesson, teachers can foster the integration of cues by employing Big Books. The following are some examples of how different checking strategies may be fostered:

1. Checking using visual cues.

Sally went to the __________ with her friend.

In this case the target word is *shop*. The teacher asks for predictions based on the meaning of the word, and then asks children what letters they would expect to see, thus fostering the use of visual cues.

2. Checking using meaning cues.

Sally w_____ to the shop.

In this case the target word is *went*. The teacher asks for predictions from the way the word looks and then invites children to check to see if it makes sense with the surrounding text.

3. Checking using structural cues.

Sally went to the shop w______ her friend.

In this case the target word is *with*. The teacher could suggest predictions based on the way the word began, for example *will, when*, and *with*. The teacher would then ask the children which one **sounded right**. Certainly *will* doesn't fit the structure, but at the stage of the substitution, *when* does. In this case children will need to read further to reject the prediction.

Of course the goal is to have the children flexible in the use of cues, and the teacher should quickly move on to combining the above steps, for example, "Can you think of a word that makes sense, sounds right, and looks right?"

Larger chunks of text require children to make more global and long term predictions. This is where *guided reading* becomes important. Because the main goal of reading anything is to make sense of what is read, children need to be continually asking questions of the text, and checking on those predictions. The role of the teacher in a *guided reading* lesson is to help children to formulate their own questions. Traditional lessons saw the teacher formulating the questions and then getting children to read part of the text to search for answers. However, this doesn't encourage children to formulate their own questions. Certainly, teacher designed questions may be appropriate in the very early stages of reading acquisition, but teachers need to quickly begin helping children to formulate their own.

Teachers can accomplish this by carefully selecting meaningful text, and introducing it in such a way that questions naturally arise. After the introduction, and perhaps a search of the first few pictures, if appropriate, teachers can then invite children to pose their own questions. Children can be encouraged to articulate their questions in front of the group, or to write them down if articulation is threatening. The group is then asked to read the text to check on their predictions. Once this is completed each child is invited to discuss what they have found out.

This is where a skilled teacher can really help children to construct more appropriate questions. Children are encouraged to decide what it was in the text that led them to confirm or reject their original predictions. The teacher's role is to *guide* the group towards better first predictions.

This approach helps children to see how their own perceptions change with new information being processed. There is an added advantage, in that the sharing process at the end helps children to understand the range of questions that can be asked of text.

Re-reading and Reading On

Children need to be encouraged to re-read text when meaning breaks down, or generally, if there is a mismatch in cues. Re-reading allows children to process print again, and to search further for cues. This is easy to model during *shared reading,* where the teacher can make intentional errors, and allow the children to join in on the re-reading. High progress readers also tend to re-read after having spent time processing text. This can also be modelled by the teacher.

Reading-on needs to be clearly defined. We are dealing with behaviour that is initiated by the child after they have made a substitution. Sometimes teachers confuse this with the process of children omitting unknown words, continuing on to the end of the sentence and then going back to try to figure out the problem word. This is not a particularly useful strategy. The child has to do too much. He or she has to hold the preceding text in short term memory, process more text, return, and then attempt to use all of this to work out the unknown word.

It is important that the child makes some substitution before continuing on. In this case, reading-on will allow the child to pick up information that they can check against the prediction. This can be modelled in *shared reading.* The teacher can choose 3 or 4 words that fit the context at the time, but where the overall meaning or structure of the rest of the sentence will allow the child to reject or confirm their prediction.

Developing Fluency and Expression

There are children who can predict and check text well, but do so slowly and without much expression. This is often the result of the teacher's thrust for precise word- perfect reading. This wish is understandable. Teachers want children to control the early strategies of left to right processing, and one to one matching. This is why finger pointing is important at the early stages of reading. When should finger pointing be discouraged? This is largely a judgment call by the experienced professional. However, when finger pointing gets in the way of fluent, meaningful reading, it becomes a problem. Lack of fluency is a major problem with children who find reading difficult, and this is addressed in a later chapter.

The teacher can encourage children to read fluently and with expression in a number of ways. Certainly *reading-to* children in an exaggerated fashion will encourage expression and model fluency. Children can also benefit from tape-assisted reading; listening to a story, read with expression and at normal speech, while they follow along with their own copy of the text. After a few training sessions, children are quite comfortable with this mode of delivery.

For more direct instruction, *shared reading* is ideal. Again, the teacher can model fluent and expressive reading as the children are encouraged to read along. For fluent reading, the teacher can use a masking card that he or she shifts from left to right, forcing the eye to move quicker. For phrasing, the teacher could divide text into meaningful phrases and have children read them with the appropriate pauses. For expression, the teacher can choose passages that include direct speech, exclamations, questions, and so on, and model how this reading would sound. Of course, teachers have always worked upon this area, but often in an incidental way. However, it is important that children start reading fluently, and with expression, as quickly as possible. The longer children read in a voice pointing mode, the harder it is to shift the behaviour.

Mileage Grouping

Children learn to read by reading, and it is critical to such a program that children have every opportunity to practice the strategies they have been developing. This is where grouping based upon "reading age" can be useful. Children need to be introduced to a range of text at their "level". *Shared* and *guided* lessons with groups of children based upon reading age will introduce children to a range of text, that they can then practice upon.

Final Note

It could be argued that such a concentration on detail takes away from the learning to read by reading concept, or that what is being proposed is not necessary for most children. These are good points of view. However, if one is going to engage in teaching, it seems appropriate that the teaching is directed towards need. If we believe that successful readers use certain strategies, and we can identify a group of children who at a particular time are not employing these strategies, it makes perfect sense to teach the required behaviour and then allow children the opportunity to practice. Chapter 3 will concentrate on making priority decisions about what to teach, and how to plan an effective program.

3. PLANNING AND THE USE OF TEACHER TIME

To plan an effective program the teacher needs to allocate time for:

- Introduction of new material (mileage grouping).
- Strategy based teaching.
- Monitoring.

Mileage Grouping or Individualised Programs

Because the more children read, the more they find out about reading, and the better they get, a reading program must provide massive opportunities for children to read meaningful text. The question of whether to group for this, or to provide individual programs, is a difficult one. On the one hand, individualised reading programs are the ultimate goal, where reading material is self-selected and monitored by the children. As teachers we should be continually working towards this. Certainly, this can be accomplished with older, more independent readers, who can keep an accurate reading log, and be discriminating in their choice of text. However, for children just beginning the process, grouping has the advantage of allowing the teacher to introduce varied genre and text styles that children at a particular level may not have encountered. Given the problems associated with the concept of reading age, children can still be loosely grouped in this way for the purpose of mileage. It can be misleading to make ultra-fine distinctions. For example, the difference between a reading age of 6 years 3 months and 6 years 4 months is largely meaningless. Teachers should be able to work within a broad range where there are no more than 5 groups.

The purpose of working with such groups is to continually introduce new text, where the challenges are manageable, and to help children to respond to text in varying ways. The teacher may decide to introduce the new material through *shared* or *guided* reading, depending on the complexity of the text. Once the material has been introduced and the children have had the opportunity to come to grips with it, the teacher may wish to model a new response, or remind children of previous responses that they have used. Children would then be free to choose a response, or read from their group box, or engage in a related reading activity.

Strategy-Based Grouping

It can not be overly stressed that strategy-based grouping should only occur when there is a clear need established. While the goal of mileage grouping is building up the quantity and variation of new text, the goal of strategy-based grouping is to foster specific reading strategies that will be common to all text. What to teach and when to teach it are tricky questions, because children learn different things at different times, and reading strategies do not follow a neat, linear progression. However, there are some overriding considerations that can be made. The difficult question to be answered for any particular child is, "What is the next learning step? What would this child most benefit from learning how to do?"

For example, children who consistently stop at unknown words, need to develop the strategy of using meaning cues to predict. The drive for meaning is paramount. Children who predict well using meaning cues, but don't check using visual cues, need to learn to do so. Children who are predicting and checking well, but processing very slowly, need to develop fluency. It is not the intention of this publication to present a recipe — to do so would be to deny the interactive nature of the reading process — however, by carefully analysing running records, a teacher can make good decisions about what to foster next.

Monitoring Reading and Making Decisions

The following are some examples of running records taken from the same text, and possible decisions that could be made, about future teaching. The passage is taken from *Where is My Caterpillar* (Noonan, 1992).

Running Record #1

That night I looked in

our garden for a bug.

I found a fat green caterpillar

on a cabbage.

This is a child who is not predicting well when confronted by unknown words. The child needs to develop a consistent use of meaning cues.

Running Record #2 Analysis

went

That night I looked in — (m) (s) v

our garden for a bug.

saw

I found a fat green caterpillar — (m) (s) v

on a cabbage.

In the second running record the child **is** using meaning and structural cues to predict unknown words, but not checking with other cue sources. The child needs to learn to re-read and check.

Running Record #3

That night I looked in

our garden for a bug .

in

I found a fat green caterpillar

on a cabbage.

The confusion here probably stems from the child completely missing the punctuation mark at the end of the second line. The child continues on, attempting to make a substitution that will maintain meaning. In this instance the child needs to learn to read the punctuation.

The above running records are contrived and the required behaviours are fairly clear. Of course, real children don't always present such straightforward pictures of their reading. However, where the behaviours are more complex, it is still possible to decide upon what to foster next.

Running Record #4

That night I looked in

bag

our garden for a bug.

big

I found a fat green caterpillar

on a cabbage.

in sc jug

I put it in a jar

beside my bed.

There is a lot of interesting behaviour here. The task is to pick out the most significant. In this case, if we go back to first principles — that the primary goal is reading for meaning — it can be seen that the substitutions of *big* for *fat* and *jug* for *jar* generally maintain the overall meaning of the passage, as does the self correction of *in* for *it*. Without looking more closely, one could be tempted to concentrate on checking strategies. However, the most critical piece of behaviour is the *bag* for *bug* substitution. This makes some sense at the sentence level, but not in the overall context of the story. In this case, the teacher would wish to foster meaning in larger segments of text.

In general, the teacher is making the best judgment based on the available data, and a knowledge of the strategies that successful readers use. It seems more reasonable to group children for this kind of instruction based upon behavioural data, than based upon reading age. This is simply because children with similar reading ages will be reading text in vastly different ways, and consequently traditional lessons will of necessity be less targeted to specific needs.

Using Teacher Time Effectively

As a fairly general rule, it is suggested that teachers spend whatever time is available for reading in the following way:

- Mileage groups: 2 x 15 minute sessions per day.
- Strategy-based groups: 1 x 15 minute session per day.
- Monitoring: 3 children (15 minutes per day).

The time allocation may need to be modified here if there is more or less time allocated for reading. Over a period of a week, this will allow the teacher to work twice with mileage groups, take strategy-based groups as the need arises, and take running records on half the class. The results of those running records will help to determine the following week's strategy-based groups. The above allocation is only a suggestion, and teachers will alter the time allocations to suit the needs of their children and their school's organisation.

A final advantage to organising monitoring and teaching in such a way, is that it will quickly become clear if there is a particular bias in a teacher's reading program that causes children to concentrate upon some strategies at the expense of others.

Record Keeping

Even in literature based programs, the traditional approach to record keeping has been a graph of growth in reading age, or book level. This is still useful in terms of summative data. Certainly, it is useful to know how far a child has moved, but this needs to be accompanied by diagnostic information.

Each school or district will have their own method of keeping and using records, and some of these will be prescribed by outside agencies. It is important to keep accurate records on how children are processing print. Age level alone can be misleading. It is quite easy to imagine a child with a reading age of 5 years 9 months using strategies in a more integrated fashion, than a child with a reading age of 6. The important information, from a planning and teaching point of view, is how each child is processing.

Checklists appear to be favoured by some teachers, but there is a tendency for these to be seen in a lock-step way. For reading, the problem with this approach is that the development of the independent use of reading strategies tends to be spiral in nature. It is not a case of developing one and then moving on to the next. Children are continually refining their use of strategies. A method of record keeping that is anecdotal and ongoing is seen as desirable, for example:

"Child 'A' at a 6 year 6 month level, appears to be predicting well using meaning and structural cues, but not always checking using visual cues; reads fluently, but without much expression."

The above passage summarises the position, and presents diagnostic information that allows the teacher to plan for appropriate teaching. Despite best intentions and superb planning, some children still have difficulty. Chapter 4 will concentrate upon this area.

4. WORKING WITH CHILDREN WHO HAVE DIFFICULTY

The Concept of Reading Difficulty

The term *difficulty* is used deliberately here as it does not set limits on the group of children affected. We are looking at helping any child who has a reading difficulty, without labelling that difficulty in any way whatsoever. A term such as *reading disability* implies a specific neurological condition, that has been diagnosed as such. There is much debate as to the usefulness of such a term, anyway. The major problem is that whether children are diagnosed with a *specific reading* or *learning disability* or not, they still need to learn to read. We need to work with any child who requires help, regardless of any assumptions made about the child. For a further discussion of this subject see Clay, 1987.

Causes and Cures

The question of why some children learn to read easily and others do not, is a fascinating and complex one. There are many reasons why some children may have considerable difficulty getting under way and why some children continue to fall further and further behind. Children come to school with various experiences that may or may not help in learning to read. Certain pre-conditions upon arrival at school may affect later learning. These can be loosely grouped as follows:

- Life experiences.
- Language experience.
- Confidence and motivation.
- Physical conditions.
- Recognition of words and letters.

Children who arrive at school with limited *life experiences* will obviously have less to bring to the task of reading. Similarly, children who have not been read to, or whose language development is somewhat lacking, will have more difficulty processing text.

To learn to read, or for that matter to learn anything, children need to have the confidence to take risks. Children who, for whatever reasons, arrive at school lacking this confidence may have more difficulty in learning to read.

Motivation is an interesting problem. It is rare to find a child who on the first day of school is not motivated to learn to read. One only needs to ask the child why they have come to school. Most will mention learning to read. However, after some time at school, this motivation may not be evident, and this is usually due to repeated failure.

Naturally, certain physical conditions to do with sight, hearing, and perhaps co-ordination, can make learning to read more difficult. Finally, children who come to school with some knowledge about words and letters will be in a better position to check their predictions.

Given the above, some children may come to school highly motivated, possessing strong language skills and positive life experiences, and still experience difficulty in learning to read. One skill may over-ride another, or the child may have difficulty putting it all together. While it is useful to consider what a child is bringing to the task, we shouldn't make too many assumptions. What is of greater concern is the temptation to delay reading instruction because of some perceived deficit. In traditional phonic or sight word approaches, a child needed to learn to read in steps, and the concept of readiness made sense. However in terms of the view of reading presented in this book, readiness makes no sense from the learners perspective. **It is the teacher who needs to be ready.** The teacher needs to decide where the child is at and adjust the program accordingly.

Maturation is another concept sometimes cited as a consideration for delaying instruction. However, because reading is a learned behaviour, the concept of maturation makes little sense. We all know of a few children who, left to their own devices, have "matured" their way into reading. The vast majority, if left alone, continue to fall further and further behind. There is no good reason for delaying reading instruction, and compelling reasons not to.

Another circumstance that causes some teachers to delay reading instruction is the attribution of specific conditions such as *dyslexia*. It is not the intention of this book to debate the term in detail; whether such a condition exists is in itself debatable. However, it is a dangerous label because the term is not clearly defined. Dyslexia assumes a neurological condition, and may make teachers feel that they need specialist knowledge to help these children. In truth, what children, rightly or wrongly diagnosed in this way need to learn, is no different from what any child needs to learn. Frank Smith puts it best:

"The cure for dyslexia is to read." (Smith, 1985, p. 152)

What we are left with are some possible reasons, or a combination of circumstances, that may contribute to children having some difficulty in learning to read. No matter what the circumstances, there is no reason to delay instruction. The above terms are of little instructional value, and may essentially become excuses for not teaching. One of the most obvious and most significant difference between successful readers and those having difficulty, is the amount of reading undertaken. If children learn to read by reading, then any delay, or engagement in tasks that do not involve reading meaningful text, will exacerbate the situation.

A Successful Intervention Model

The Reading Recovery program (Clay, 1985) developed in New Zealand, and now gaining increasing respect and usage in other countries, is an example of a successful intervention program for children having difficulty in the early stages of literacy learning. The program aims to help children who have had one year of literacy instruction and who: require further direct instruction in the techniques and strategies for interacting with text, additional experience with the forms and structure of text, and a low risk learning environment, in order to read successfully. Typically, these children are chosen from those who comprise the lowest test score group based on a series of diagnostic tests developed by Marie Clay for this purpose, regardless of any other factors.

The program is highly successful, in a variety of cultural settings, for a number of reasons. These include:

- Careful diagnosis.
- Early intervention.
- Individualised programs.
- Thorough post-program monitoring.

Teachers are thoroughly trained in Reading Recovery procedures and receive ongoing support after their initial training. Ideally, if the program was fully implemented, and every child who needed help had access to it, this chapter would not be necessary. However, under present conditions, it is not always possible to provide specialist help to all the children who require it. It is important for two reasons that classroom teachers feel confident about being able to work in this area. First, for whatever reasons, teachers will continue to have children in their class who are experiencing some difficulty. Second, teachers will be better able to support the efforts of specialists if they have some common understanding of the ongoing needs of children with reading difficulties.

The Role of the Classroom Teacher

The remainder of this chapter will concentrate upon the diagnosis of children requiring further help, constructing an effective program, and the important issue of finding time to work with individual children. Although the information presented has some obvious similarities to Reading Recovery, there is no intention that it could ever replace this dynamic and successful approach. It could be argued, that this approach is an unsatisfactory application of a program designed to be used with highly trained teachers working with young children. While sympathising with that position, we continue to have children in our classrooms who have difficulty with reading, and the issue needs to be addressed.

Diagnosis

There are a number of assessment measures applied in a variety of settings, from nationally based assessment, through to individual teacher-based assessment. Whatever the measure, or set of measures used, it needs to reflect a consistent view of the reading process. If we believe that children learn to read by reading, then we need to assess children in the act of reading. This requires the use of running records of reading behaviour. A carefully analysed set of running records taken at easy, instructional, and difficult text levels, will yield useful information about what the child is able to do and what he or she needs to learn to do.

It is suggested that the running records, where possible, should be taken on seen material. This is especially important with older children, where the reading age of unseen material may be more a function of interest and background knowledge. In addition to the running records, it is useful to have information on word recognition, and a sample of writing/spelling behaviour. This information can then be used to build a profile of where the child is at. Selection of the children in need will not usually be a problem for the teacher who is already keeping useful diagnostic records. However, if this is not the case, it is suggested that teachers assess at least the lower third of their class, as "gut-feeling" is often misleading.

In summary, it is useful to build a profile that includes the following:

- A running record at an easy level (>95% accuracy).
- A running record at instructional level (90-95% accuracy).
- A running record at a difficult text level (<90% accuracy).
- A measure of high frequency word knowledge.
- A measure of writing/spelling performance.

In addition, a check on eyesight and hearing records is essential. With the above information, the teacher is now able to construct an appropriate program.

Constructing a Program

In general, children who are experiencing some difficulty with reading require a program that is similar to that of their classmates, but more concentrated. There is the temptation to work on the assumption that since these children have had difficulty with learning from a specific method, they need something quite different. Except in extreme cases, where the help of a specialist may be required, this is not usually the case.

Because children learn to read by reading, any program catering for the needs of children having difficulty requires a major component of meaningful text reading. A suggested program would include the following:

- Familiar reading.
- Writing.
- Introduction of new reading material.

Familiar Reading

The purpose of having the child exposed to massive amounts of text, is to build up mileage, and to allow the child the opportunity to practice the strategies he or she uses well on material that does not present too much of a challenge. The choice of reading materials will depend upon what the child has been exposed to, and especially with older children, what they are interested in. The role of the teacher is to help assemble this material and to set it aside for the exclusive use of this particular child.

Depending on available time, the role of the teacher is to support the child as he or she reads the text. It is important for the teacher to be thoroughly familiar with the appropriate strategies the child uses, and those which he or she needs to acquire. As the child is reading, the teacher is looking for opportunities to positively reinforce appropriate behaviours, and model necessary strategies.

This support procedure may only require 5 or 10 minutes of the teacher's time. Where time is at a premium, as it usually is, it is sometimes possible to train others to provide appropriate feedback. These could include teacher aides, parents and caregivers, and even other children.

After the instructional time, children need to be encouraged to continue reading from their store of material. This of course is harder to monitor, and some children may not build the desired mileage. One way to overcome this is through tape-assisted reading. This is a method employing either commercially produced audio cassettes, or better still, teacher produced tapes of familiar material. With this method, the child chooses the cassette of the story he or she wishes to read, and then follows along reading the text. This quickly builds reading mileage, and helps develop fluency.

Writing

Writing is an important component in the reading process, as the skills in writing complement those in reading. Certainly this area helps develop the use of visual cues for checking when reading text. For some children, it can be the key to unravelling the reading difficulty.

Often, children who have difficulty with reading, also have difficulty with written language. The amount of writing that the child completes in any one session may be minimal, and certainly will depend upon what age group is being focused on. However, it is the quality of what is written, and the learning that takes place, that is important. During the writing time, it is the teacher's role to encourage the child to write a "story". Although some children can be reluctant to begin, and state they have nothing to write about, it is important for the teacher to use all his or her skills and cunning to elicit a story that comes from the child. The reason for this is that with a child-generated story, the child doesn't need to concentrate further on meaning and structural cues, and can focus attention on going from sound to letter. It is also important that the child has a complete sentence in mind before beginning to write. This helps avoid the piece by piece construction of meaning, that can overburden the process.

Throughout the writing session, the teacher helps the child in a number of ways. It becomes a shared task with the teacher taking over the writing when it becomes difficult for the child. The teacher needs to help the child to:

- Build up a store of high frequency words.
- Extend the length and complexity of stories.
- Use what is known about the ways in which words are constructed to help with new words.

Words that the child can nearly spell need to be taken to fluency and continually revised. There is the danger that children will become too comfortable with a small writing vocabulary, and tend to use and re-use these words in future stories. The teacher needs to help extend the writing vocabulary, by showing connections between what is known about words and how this can be used to generate new words. Strategies teachers might employ to for this are: simply to encourage children to "have a go", look for patterns, see relationships in word structures, and group words by patterns, not themes.

New Reading Material

While the reading of familiar material helps to build some mileage and to practice strategies, there is the need to continually develop the flexible use of these strategies on new and different types of text. The choice of material will depend upon what strategy the teacher wishes to foster. The extent to which the book is introduced, and the degree of emphasis, will also depend upon this. The goal of the introduction is to give the child enough information to enable him or her to read successfully with some assistance. Throughout the introduction and subsequent reading, the teacher takes the opportunity to model behaviours he or she wishes the child to learn. The behaviours to be fostered will be established through the ongoing analysis of running records that are taken throughout the program.

During the program it is important for teachers to keep up-to-date records of strategies used and required in both reading and writing.

The issue of finding time to work with individual children is a difficult one. It is often counter-productive to set aside time during breaks, as this can be viewed negatively by the child, and can also put undue stress upon the teacher. There are a few ways to get around this. The teacher could structure his or her reading time in such a way as to free up 5 or 10 minutes daily. If this is difficult, then perhaps the teacher could find some time during another curriculum area. If this is still a problem, the teacher can delegate at least some of the task to parents, teacher aides or other children, as long as they are suitably trained. Finally, in cases where there is a team approach to teaching, some reciprocal arrangement can be made. Different arrangements will suit different teachers. For some it will be easier than for others.

However, in the case where specialist help is unavailable or unwarranted, and finding time is difficult, there is still a child in need of help, and as professionals we need to find some way of providing that assistance.

5. TEACHING THE TEACHERS

Any program is more likely to be successful if it is consistent over time and space. This chapter discusses the importance of helping others use natural language texts and a strategy-based approach in their teaching of reading.

Establishing Your Own Program

Before enthusiastically embarking on a conversion crusade, it is essential to feel that one's own program is running successfully. Look at the ongoing running records and the careful records that have been kept. Check to see if the children are:

- Using appropriate strategies in a consistent manner.
- Reading increasingly more difficult text.
- Reading a wider range of genre.
- Responding to text in varied and imaginative ways.
- Generally showing enthusiasm for reading.

Next, look at yourself. Are you comfortable with your teaching? Is planning and/or monitoring too time consuming? Are you committed to this way of working? If there are problems in this area, it is suggested that the teacher reviews the situation, in order to minimise the problem. Often, difficulties are a result of trying to do too much, too quickly. Take some time out. Don't teach. Watch the children as they read and respond. You may be pleasantly surprised. You may find you need to do less teaching, allowing children more time to practice appropriate reading strategies.

It is only when you are comfortable with the progress the children are making, and with your own teaching, that it is time to broaden the approach to your colleagues.

The Target Group

To ensure maximum consistency, the goal is to have the entire school running a strategy-based program. In most cases the key individual to begin talking with, is the school principal. For some, this will be a daunting task. They are usually very busy people, dedicated to educational excellence, who have to satisfy the needs and wishes of a very diverse group, ranging from the government, to the consumer. It is critical to keep these circumstances in mind when making the initial approach.

Most principals are interested in results. In the initial meeting, present the material you have been carefully accumulating. Present it in graph form; be succinct. Allow the results to speak for themselves.

Most principals will wish to see the program in action. Invite the principal into your classroom during reading time. Invite him or her to observe lessons, talk with children, and sample the children's responses. The principal will be impressed, both with what the children are doing, and your confidence in the approach.

Principals are also concerned with meeting established assessment criteria. It will be very important for the teacher to assure the principal that standardised measures can still be applied. What needs to be stressed is that, while the necessary cumulative records can still be kept, a strategy-based approach also allows for a diagnostic analysis that will improve teaching and learning.

Cost, of course, is also a consideration. A whole language approach allows for the use of a huge range of material, that can be selected to reflect the social and cultural needs of the children at a particular school, eliminating high and untargetted expenditure.

Principals will be concerned with the effect of innovation on the parents and caregivers of the children. It is important to assure the principal that this is an area that will be addressed early on the in the adoption of the strategy-based program (see Morrison, 1993).

Finally, principals are concerned with the effect of innovation on other staff members. Therefore the teacher should come to the initial meeting with the names of two or three other teachers who are interested in hearing more. Above all, start small.

If the teacher has done his or her homework, is committed to the program, and successfully anticipated the possible concerns of the principal, the meeting should be a success. The next step is working with the teachers.

Working with Staff

It can not be stressed enough that the teacher needs to start with a small group of colleagues who at least show some interest in the approach. Change in education can be incredibly slow, although sometimes this is for the best.

A teacher will need to plan for a number of sessions over a period of at least a term. This number will vary greatly with the understanding and commitment of the group. The following is one possible approach to staff training.

General Introduction

More than likely, the teachers who have shown an interest in the program will already know that something different is going on in your classroom. An ideal introduction is to arrange for those interested to be released for a short time, to observe the children and the program. Because your program is running so well, the visit will naturally create interest, and preliminary questions about planning, methods and assessment can be explored. Some teachers, however, may be quite sceptical. This attitude could well work against success. It is recommended that you invite only those who remain reasonably enthusiastic to a preliminary meeting, at a time that is convenient to all.

The Preliminary Meeting

The goal of this meeting is to enlist long-term support and effort, so it needs to be carefully planned. You are in a strong position because you are enthusiastic, the teachers have seen the success in your classroom, and you have the necessary records to back this up. Your major difficulty may be with teachers wishing to change overnight. They may also be more interested in the *how* than the *why*. Your role in this first session is to convince teachers that this is an ongoing process that requires some understanding of theory, and that this understanding will make for stronger, more consistent teaching. Establish a firm list of dates — perhaps once a week — throughout the term. The number of meetings will depend upon what the teachers are bringing to the task. Major sessions will need to highlight theory, assessment, reading strategies, and planning. These factors will need to be continually linked.

The Reading Theory Session

This session needs to be handled carefully. The mere mention of *theory* can have a negative effect. However, it is be the cornerstone of any good reading program, and should be reflected in all facets of planning, teaching and evaluation.

The theory session needs to be kept light, but the message about how children learn to read needs to be clear. Start from where teachers are at. Ask for their views on how children learn to read, and especially, how they know. Collect the suggestions and have them prominently displayed. Use these suggestions to build a continuum from top-down to bottom-up approaches (see Morrison, 1993). Ensure that teachers are clear about the differences in the models. There may be a wide range of opinion here. It is important to accept that range, and leave it on hold, while exploring the "how do you know?" question.

The most convincing arguments often result from teachers reflecting upon their own reading habits. Often, a combination of a simple but cleverly constructed cloze exercise, and a passage where teachers can read all the words but not get to the meaning of the text, is sufficient to start shifting teachers towards the importance of language structure, and pre-knowledge; that is, what they are bringing to the task.

Equally important, is getting teachers to look carefully at behavioural data on successful beginning readers.

What needs to become clear by the end of the session(s) is that successful beginning readers use what they know about the world, and the language patterns they have developed, to help them decode meaningful text. If necessary, audio-tape high progress readers, or better still invite teachers into the classroom to observe.

The "Real Books" Session

Once it has been firmly established that what children bring to the task is critical in reading, it is a simple step to establish the importance of using material that makes sense and contains natural language. Although it seems self-evident, to highlight the point, the teacher could bring along a range of material; phonic based, look-say, natural language, and so on, and invite the group to explore the limitations certain types of material put on the use of what the child is already bringing to the task. Some teachers may still argue that, without controlled text, one can not plan appropriate learning steps. This is the ideal time to introduce the use of running records.

The Running Records Session

Teachers need to feel they can begin to take running records of reading behaviour before they have thoroughly mastered all the intricacies. Since monitoring the child's reading behaviour is the key to future planning, the teachers may need to spend considerable time on this, perhaps spread-out throughout the term. For a basic outline of how to take running records, refer to the Appendix.

An appropriate beginning session would involve the taking and scoring of running records. Audio-tapes are useful here. They are favoured over *live* children, as it is easier to control the situation. Teachers need to be comfortable with the idea that they may hear things slightly differently from their colleagues, however this will not excessively change the overall profile.

Once teachers are comfortable with the mechanics of running records, they can be introduced to the analysis of cues. Again teachers need to feel confident, so it is important to keep things simple. Use the same running records used for the mechanics, and invite teachers to look at each miscue and ask the following questions:

- Does it make sense within the context of the story?
- Does it sound right? (is it the same part of speech?)
- Does the word look similar?

For self-corrections, ask the same questions for the original miscue, and then ask:

- Given the answer to the above, why did the child make the correction?

Teachers need to do the analysis quickly, and not get bogged down in detail. They also need to understand that even though their analysis may vary slightly from that of others, it will not greatly change the overall profile.

Finally, when teachers are beginning to feel more comfortable with the analysis of cues, one can start to delve deeper into the use of strategies. The goal is not only to get teachers comfortable with this area, but to be using the language and terminology appropriate to the program.

The Planning Sessions

Hopefully, teachers will already be taking and analysing running records, and looking for significant behaviours. Now is the time to introduce the concepts of *strategy* and *mileage* based grouping. As before, take this slowly. Emphasise the need to only group for strategy-based teaching, when there is a clear reason for doing so. It is probably a good idea to model sample lessons, either using a contrived situation or having teachers observe in your classroom.

Reviewing the Process

Throughout this training period there will be the need for constant review. Some teachers may begin to falter, while others may revel in the success of the program. Careful monitoring and encouragement will be essential. Teachers will not be convinced of the value of strategy-based teaching until they have experienced success. Once they have, you will have a group of committed colleagues, and will be in a much stronger position to work on the rest of the school.

6. CONCLUSION

The goal of this book has been to help those teachers who are considering, or are at least beginning to think about, a strategy-based approach to the teaching of reading. A number of issues have been considered and discussed.

However, this book is not meant as a recipe. It is fully recognised that some teachers will be well on the way towards strategy-based teaching, and others will find this a totally new approach. It is also recognised that implementing such a program will be easier in some situations than in others.

Very few people in education have the autonomy to make program decisions without consulting with others, and perhaps this is for the best. We need to be thoroughly convinced that what we are doing is educationally sound and in the best interests of the children. It is a combination of success, enthusiasm, and the ability to articulate the underlying theory, that will go a long way towards convincing even the most sceptical administrators of the worth of strategy-based teaching.

Finally, don't rush things. Children, parents and administrators will need time to get used to the new approach. You will need time to review and adjust the program as you become more confident. Keep faith in the fact that children learn to read by reading.

7. SUGGESTED READINGS

Children's Texts Used

Noonan, D. *Where is My Caterpillar*? Lands End Publishing, 11 Parliament Street, Lower Hutt, New Zealand, 1993

References

Clay, Marie. *The Early Detection of Reading Difficulties: A Diagnostic Survey with Recovery Procedures.* 3rd ed. Portsmouth N.H.:Heinemann,1985

Clay, Marie. "Learning to be Learning Disabled" in *NZ Journal of Educational Studies*, Vol 22, No 2, 1987

Goodman, K.S. *Miscue Analysis: Applications to Reading Instruction.* ERIC Clearinghouse on Reading and Communication Skills; National Council of Teachers of English. 1111 Kenyon Road, Urbana Illinois, 1973

Morrison, I. *Getting it Together: Linking Reading Theory to Practice*. Lands End Publishing, 11 Parliament St., Lower Hutt, New Zealand, 1993

Smith, F., *Reading* 2nd ed. Cambridge, United Kingdom: Cambridge University Press, 1985

Glossary

Ability Grouping
The grouping of children with similar needs for instructional purposes. These groups should be constantly adjusted, in response to the changing needs of children.

Balanced Language Program
A quality literacy program that encompasses the best approaches for oral, written, and visual language.

Comprehension
The interpretation of the print on the page into a meaningful message. This will depend on the reader's prior knowledge, cultural and social background, and their ongoing comprehension monitoring strategies.

Cues
Readers integrate several sources of information, or cues, to monitor ongoing reading comprehension.

Guided Reading
Students work in ability groups to read as independently as possible a text that you have selected for them and introduced to them. This text will be at the students' instructional level: the students will be able to read it with 90-94% accuracy.

Independent Reading
Students engage in independent reading (95-100% accuracy) daily, in order to build reading "mileage".

Phonological Cues
Readers use their knowledge of letter/sound and sound/letter relationships to predict and confirm reading.

Reading Levels
Independent: 95-100% accuracy
Instructional: 90-94% accuracy
Frustrational: 89% or less accuracy

Record of Reading Behaviour
A neutral observation during which you record, using a standard set of symbols, everything the child says as s/he reads a book you have chosen.

Semantic Cues
Readers use their prior knowledge, sense of the story, and pictures to assist with prediction and confirmation of the meaning of text.

Syntactic Cues
Readers use their oral language and prior knowledge of how language works (e.g., word order) to assist with prediction and confirmation of text.

Appendix

The Record of Reading Behaviour

The record of reading behaviour is based on the work of Marie Clay and Kenneth Goodman, who pioneered the concept of close observation of children's reading behaviour, especially as it relates to the types of miscues children make as they read.

Steps for taking the record

1. Selecting the text
The text you choose for the record will depend on your purpose. For instance, if you want to see how well a child is reading at his or her current instructional level, you will choose a book that the child has already read. If you want to see if the child is able to cope with more difficult material, you will choose a book from current instructional level that the child has not seen before.

2. Introducing the text
Children should be given an introduction to any text that they are being asked to read to help them make sense of the author's message. Before taking a record on a story that the child has read before, you may need to do no more than introduce the text by supplying the title. If the child is unfamiliar with the book, you should give the child the title and a one- or two-sentence summary of the plot and theme. For example: "This is a story called *Buster McCluster*. It's about a

man who planted some sprouts and didn't watch for bugs. When he cooked them, all the bugs popped out and gave his wife a fright." If the story contains any particularly difficult syntax or vocabulary, some account of these should be incorporated in your introduction.

3. Taking the record

Choose a passage of 100 to 150 words (unless the entire book contains fewer words). Sit the child beside you so that you can see the text. Some teachers like to photocopy the text so they can make notations on a copy of the text. If using photocopies, be careful not to get into the habit of fitting the child to the text that you have photocopied, rather than using material that is appropriate to the child. Where children are experiencing difficulties, it is easier to record their efforts on a blank record of reading behaviour, rather than be constrained by the small space afforded by a photocopy of the text.

After your introduction, the child should read the text independently. You must resist all temptations to teach while you are taking the record, as any intervention except telling the child an unknown word will distort the interpretation of the record. You need to remember that you are looking closely at what children can do by themselves.

While the child reads the text, you will use the suggested notation to record all the reading behaviours that the child exhibits. At points of error, always note the child's response on top and the text below. While you are learning, use a pencil, space the check marks well while still matching them to the number of words on the line, and write down as much as possible of what the child says. You can always fill in the text later. You may also wish to tape the reading for further reference. As you become more proficient with your observations, you will notice more and more behaviours. Practice is the key to success.

4. Retelling the story

To check the child's level of comprehension in relation to the plot, the setting, the characters, and any underlying inferences, you should invite the child to retell the story in his or her own words when they have completed the reading. You may need to follow this retelling with questions to elicit further information.

5. Calculating the reading level and the self-correction rate

The purpose of calculating the reading level is to tell you if the book is at a level at which the child can read independently, or with guidance, or if it is at a level which will merely frustrate the child. An accurate score of 95-100% suggests that the child is able to read this and any material of similar difficulty easily and independently. The purpose of calculating the self-correction rate is to give you some guidance as to how well the child is able to both notice and correct errors during reading.

An accuracy score of 90-94% suggests that this text and texts at a similar level will present challenges that the child will be increasingly able to control with your guidance in an instruction reading situation. An accuracy score of less than 89% suggests that the material you have chosen is too hard for the child to control alone and that you should use such material in a shared reading situation or that you should read it to the child.

6. Scoring the record

Substitutions, insertions, omissions, and teacher-told responses score as errors. Repetitions are not scored as errors. Corrected responses are scored as self-corrections.

There is no penalty for attempts that end in a correct response:

<u>w w went</u>
went

Multiple, unsuccessful attempts at a word score as one error only:

<u>will we when</u>
went

If there are alternative ways of scoring, credit the child with the fewest errors. The lowest score for any page is zero.

If a child omits a line or lines, each word omitted is counted as an error. If the child omits a page, deduct the number of words omitted from the number of words that you have used off the record. If the child repeatedly makes an error with a proper noun (the name of a person or a place), count this as an error the first time only. All other incorrect responses count as errors each time:

Paul
Peter — if repeated five times counts as one error

whereas

looks
looked — if repeated five times would count as five errors.

Pronunciation differences are not counted as reading errors unless accompanied by incorrect locating responses.

7. Steps in calculating the reading level
Note the number of errors made on each line on the record of reading behaviour in the column marked E. Total the number of errors in the text and divide this into the number of words that the child has read. This will give you an error rate. For example, if the child read 100 words and made 10 errors, the error rate would be 1 in 10. Convert this to an accuracy percentage using the Error Rate/Accuracy Percentage Table, and fill in the appropriate box on the record of reading behaviour.

8. Steps in calculating the self-correction rate
Note the number of self-corrections in each line in the column marked SC on the record of reading behaviour, and total them. Add the number of errors to the number of self-corrections and divide by the number of self-corrections. For example, if the child makes 10 errors and 5 self-corrections:

$\frac{(10 + 5)}{5} = \frac{15}{5}$ 1:3

Thus for every 15 errors made, 5 were corrected, which gives a self-correction rate of 1 in 3. Or put another way, the child corrected 1 of every 3 errors made. A self-correction rate of 1 in 3 to 1 in 5 is considered good and tells you that the child is not only noticing, but is able to do something about discrepancies while reading.

Analysing the record

The purpose of analysing the record of reading behaviour is to enable you to draw together a picture of reading behaviour related to the processes involved in getting meaning from print. From this analysis, you can adjust and monitor your teaching program.

There can be several outcomes from this analysis:

- A certain strategy might become the focus of a class or group shared-book experience. For example, you may find that you had to tell some of the children many of the words in the text. During your next shared-book lesson, you will be able to model effective strategies for figuring out unknown words.
- A group of children at different stages of reading acquisition, who have common needs, could be formed. For example, you may find that some children are reading in a stilted word-by-word manner. You can draw these children from across a range of reading abilities to give them extra practice in reading fluently.
- You could institute different teaching emphases for children reading at the same level of difficulty. Your records may show that some children read very fluently and accurately but are unable to retell the

story adequately. Other children may have a good grasp of the meaning, but stumble over some of the decoding. These two groups will require different instruction even though they are reading at the same level.

- You may like to take a more balanced approach to the teaching of reading. If you find that most of your children exhibit only the same narrow range of strategies when reading text independently, it may suggest that the focus of your teaching has been on these, rather than a wider, more balanced approach.

RECORD OF READING BEHAVIOUR

Name:	**Title:**
Age:	**Series:** **Seen**
Date: / /	**Stage:** **Unseen**

Calculations
Error Rate $\frac{RW}{E}$ = 1:
Accuracy %
S/C Rate $\frac{(E + SC)}{SC}$ = 1:
Level: Easy Instr Hard

Understanding from Retelling/Questioning			
Characters	Yes	....	No
Setting	Yes	....	No
Plot	Yes	....	No
Inferences	Yes	....	No

Competencies (circle predominant behaviours)			
1 on 1 matching	Directionality		Fluent Reading
At an unknown word			
Makes no attempt	Seeks help	Reruns	Reads on
Attempts using	Letter/sound knowledge	Meaning	Syntax
After an error			
Ignores	Seeks help	Reruns	Attempts s/c
Self-corrects using	Letter/sound knowledge	Meaning	Syntax

	E	**SC**	**E** **msv**	**SC** **msv**

Record of Reading Behaviour (continued)

			Cues used	
	E	**SC**	**E**	**SC**
TOTAL				

Steps in analysing the record

1. For each error and self-correction, read the sentence up to the point of error and ask yourself what led the child to make this mistake. Try to determine if the child was using cues from the meaning (semantics), the structure of the language (syntax), the visual information contained in the print (graphophonics), or a combination of these.

2. For each self-correction, ask yourself what led the child to correct this error.

3. Look to see which cue(s) the child uses predominantly. As you analyse each child's subsequent records, you will see patterns emerging that show you how well the child is integrating cues.

4. Look at the child's behaviour at an unknown word. Does the child make no attempt, seek your help, reread, read on, or make some attempt using one or more of the cues? Circle the predominant behaviour on the record of reading behaviour.

5. Follow the same procedure to see what the child typically does after an error. Circle the predominant behaviour on the record of reading behaviour.

7. Follow the same procedure to see what the child typically does after an error. Circle the predominant behaviour.

8. If the child is still reading at the emergent level, note directionality and one-to-one matching behaviours.

9. Note the child's understanding of, and memory for, the characters, setting, plot and inferences. The ability to retell at least three-quarters of the story, either unaided or in response to your questions is considered adequate.

10. Draw all this information together and write your teaching focus for this child in the box labelled "teaching strategies".